The Happiness Experiment

ahsahta press

The New Series

number 18

The Happiness Experiment

Lisa Fishman

AHSAHTA PRESS

Boise State University • Boise • Idaho • 2007

Ahsahta Press, Boise State University
Boise, Idaho 93725
http://ahsahtapress.boisestate.edu

Printed in the United States of America
Cover design by Quemadura
Author photo by Jane Williams
Book design by Janet Holmes
First printing March 2007
ISBN-13: 978-0-916272-94-4
ISBN-10: 0-916272-94-X

Library of Congress Cataloging-in-Publication Data

Fishman, Lisa, 1966-
The happiness experiment / Lisa Fishman.
    p. cm. -- (The new series ; no. 18)
ISBN-13: 978-0-916272-94-4 (alk. paper)
ISBN-10: 0-916272-94-X (alk. paper)
I. Title.

PS3556.I814572H37 2007
811'.54--DC22

                    2006024575

Acknowledgments

Poems or portions of the poems in this book were first published in magazines and, in
many cases, have been revised and/or retitled since. I thank the editors of *26: a journal
of poetry and poetics, American Letters & Commentary, Colorado Review, Conduit, Court
Green, Crazyhorse, Cutbank, Five Fingers Review, GutCult, Konundrum, mem, Mirage,
Phoebe, Poetry Salzburg Review, Shade, Slope, Verse.*

Contents

Midsummer

Suffer the lilies they do not grow
without temptation to a surface
made of water made of air

        In the Gregorian calendar
the year moved ahead ten days
the Archer moves into the Goat
sooner now   the warming globe
not hurrying

I was Esquire of the Body to Elizabeth
I was a dog-friendly motel
I was a hill of salt on the flats
        a billiard ball, a stoat

I spy something gray and green
Three gray geese in the green grass grazing

        made of opal made of ash

Off with a pinecone in your pants
you veer to the end, a side
show, a backward sleep
of all we restive in the meadow
        spun to topcoats, wept the Queen

"She and her nine fold"
means she had nine children
whereas the three of us have only one
Siamese cat with a twin
sister like a different
name between us

A canary
in the granary
made the white wheat (ripe wheat)
quiver, like eels put in the pastry pie alive

It doesn't matter if you dreamed it,
I have laundry on the line—a yellow blanket,
4 of Diamonds in a black suit,
several ardent bowls of fruit

Someone's brother "buttered his hay,"
the glossed text read, the child to
the secret flew as crow to scrap of silver in the nettles,
dove to take the rooftop of the mouth-
like Coliseum, blackbird to the snipping, four and twenty

mirrors in the room. I see she
plain as day. Did not
feed the horses, odder daughter

double the twine,
duck's in the straw
and measure nine fold from the shadow
of the cat's tail on the rafter

sweep the feathers, gently now
unthread the broom

The Ace of Bells resembles a pear
in confluence or past alarm
about the weedy berries

>*Adults are flower-feeding*
>*as the Tumbling Flower Beetle*
>*with somewhat iridescent pubescence*

With streamers in the acres scare the birds,
the bat's in the bell

>*Some are in rotting wood, others are miners*
>*of leaf and stem*
>*They are able to jump as well*

The dark downstairs resembles a stranger
on a trampoline   Most larvae are carnivorous
The cat tipped over the future

Something unconditional
apparently laid by
How look you
to the storm, to greed upon the corn

How are you so the Cantos
of Mutabilitie, myself and myselves
Article Seven
egg-in-the-tin

An ivory latch, a covered door
detain us in the field
yet we have not received the letter
explaining who and who

fell through the pineboughs like a needle
nest, come Lear again
Someone ties the grapes to wire, another turns

the clover under, upside down
we find the seedcake in the pan

A man cutting limbs in the box elder
did not saw the branch he stood on
      Purr the cat is gray
Yes, I will not stop with you
in the cataract (the web and the pin)
      All berries will be eaten
by the knave of ladders on his tractor
warning of thieves
      Suum, mun, nonny:
"this is the noise of the wind," we learn
and "('things' = penises)." Shorter maids
were daughters close in birth and darkling
the black walnut, in slander undertaken
      for to frighten, hie thee home

The locust appears harmless
in a round room, under your dress

The Dancer Orchid resembles a boy
with yellow skirt flared out as if a window

could be made of straw, Tess cuts the grass
The noted weed

you see don't worry when you close your eyes
It's only a cabbage moth, magnified many times

The phlox with no people in it
followed the afternoon: I, June, take you, July

where Bruno entered the city
in memory houses increasing
under the blindfold as worms under a stone,
ears (not tongues) of Rumour, her glorious head

I, June, take you, May, poor broody hen the dog sucks eggs
like a queen at breakfast in a poison dress

Her coat will shine from the oil
Her dress will match her hair

On a pin's head the houses collapse
into smaller houses, larger rooms
to gallop down and through for treason

makes village bells ring backward, means touch me here
who tied to her body pots and pans
for clanging, for carrying

uphill behind the town, the town a telescope
All flecks like flocks dispersing
all Catherine wheels in the corn

Someone wrote white flower
for "white flour"
on the grocery list that day

"On Tower Hill the scaffold stands out very plain"
as any three people in love
on Wood Street / on Bread Street

Friday Street / Milk
the names out of the book

January they sowed their pulse
April they poled their hops
June their horse had the botts

Planted pear trees on Dec. 31st
Carried wood-ash to the meadow / some of the house
had blown away

& children raised beside the Bridge
of Three Ships bobbing in the harbor
loaded with wine to trade for

stone for building, glass for staining
greyhounds for breeding
pigs & hens

Ducks undreamed are raucous in the morning
and the wind or laundry full of leaves

A while ago

An island is a land is not a man
upon the river in the reeds

You make a letter and so it goes   you Winter

absent how hath been

a dish of doves on offer
in a resurrection stew

or +++ ¢ ¢ ¢ for Shelley
had a notebook full of sums

Na ni ni na he wrote when he couldn't hear

the feather being held up by a mirror

Imaginary cake
    so light it floats away
    like a wedding

    or a feather
    above the dead man's mouth

    if he breathes, it stays aloft

See above
    the bird
    is a bride

    with an e next to her
    like a lover rolled up in a curve

See Lear

Howl

Here you

are, and I, *whirr*

The sunflower hung over its shadow, the sun
thinking shadow, the sun

The flowerhead was made of seeds, the seedbed
ringed with petals   something fled

I broke the flowerhead in two
like a loaf of bread or honeycomb, in two

The seeds were full of seeds
I said thinking shell, saying seed

A remark he wrote in the sun

Something came close
to coming close   Some horses
were burned I heard

and the rider, the sailor
the flowerhead flung to earth

Moon over the silo, concordance
to plant life written out by hand
by Anyone the Onion Thief
waiting out the Ides of March—
he chose the crocus and the hog,
he held apart the door
            Moon over the smokestacks,
a single hill, the steps break down
Too much movement of the infant
in the weeks before being born

There is (I have) no idea about the birch tree
or that streetlamp speck of bone chip in the road
resembling, the birds caw too
            Swiftly now, the onion thief
lays burlap over rootstock
of the medlar—keep it covered
like a cookbook or a coal

Twelve

Instructions/Confessions

Then raid the larder of licorice

Then leave the gun where you found it
in the woods behind the house

Then peel off some birch bark
to save it for paper and lose it

among the hairpins on your mother's shelf

Then find the accounts of the body
in Anäis Nin's two volumes

One for pleasure, one for sorrow

Then sing for your supper
down among the willows

wearing many buttons
on your two white blouses

Oscura Selva

The child has one body, including the mother's
Robin-body in the Rose-water, who is richer
than the owl, who is who?

The child has one body
and five words to memorize

The Queen is in a rowboat, forgetting her two bodies
Including the mother, an echo's rooms are five

Who is at the theater
designed around the doors
How very many names you have when you are loved

But it was a story about the leaves
you were turned to

But it was not the leaves you were listening
to and fro

        Still I remember
the altered figment: goat on a trampoline,
mule in a field   You should keep going
into the tree

You should have known it is singular,
that pattern of leaves the child sees

oh the idea of elephants washing
one two three four
you forgot to shut the

sleep like words for shadowed forest
resembling obscured selvcs
When suddenly I found myself
the middle of an age

When 2 people went in the water
a path opened up through the trees

one awake and one to sleep
in my arms my own
divining rod of a birdbone, never shoes

October

Dragonflies harbor a color
kept in a lamp in the meadow

Some daughters were birds and the brother
one couldn't remember

I lost the name of my mother
in the forest of its turning

Each theater a matter
twinned and rung

Questions for the Beloved at the Cow Pond

Swimming out I got wound up in weeds, the water dark
and green except the body parts it

When one of us alternates
between time & space, the rest of us
drive by the airport

Continued

Look at the moon
we sweep the porch
to look at the moon

Also pictures
without singing, out-with singing

Someone is lying
on the television
through his teeth

Once my mother had a necklace
in her dresser drawer
       child-I found it
was a square medallion
on a leather cord

Many books will answer
such a question
for example an onion / some apples

Littoral

The twin tulips planted or scattered grow
beside the bucket in a bedroom with no walls
and thou in love entirely all day

      A woman with a greenhouse
comes to mind

She might be driving down the market
She might be pointing out seals

Awake

There had been clouds across the moon
before we walked outside
      Niccolo was ilario
in his stroller: what was funny was the moon
shining off his big bald head

Myth

It all came toward
a taut moment
a snowing rain
a little rotten
apple on the branch
The girl did grow
into a tree
The lover knelt
in leafmeal I
held him in my eye

Birdcalls

The letters facing backward on construction paper,
an ꓘ or an ꙅ,
had given you a measure of a greeting

Is the hormone like an orange blossom
or the tulips' edges ragged after storms
because I wanted to risk being in general

among the stars weeds cars
and Whooping Cranes across the water really are
en route to further north and really are
"jet-black wingtipped otherwise pure"

In the really nice weather I have to lie down
like a complaint or huge glass bottle in the field
Emphatic, two-note *flee-see,*
flee-see

Acadian Flycatcher not
Arcadian
See second syllable higher in pitch

see in the stocking an accidental hole
tap tap the reason
for leaving in parts

The Fall

The raspberries are very sad
tomorrow in the field

about your body as if light
in chiaroscuro showed you things

in many ways, the light and dark
of it, in shadow or the nape of it,

each the other in among
the first and fallen make the last.

Like you staying bit
by bit or trying

on new weeds, oracular
in these. And said, we.

The Fall, Also

There were 2 trees, little one.

And looked away.

Stupid moon.

Eighth Month

Now that you're here I can fall asleep
just resting in a different place

We saw the ice floe breaking
and the river without color, only snow
as it was, and the water in the cleaving as it wasn't.

In a new black coat the ducks appear
more like a new black cape in curving
down beyond the snowline of the river. Completely
one must lie in order to.

Had walked this far around the water
when the fact appeared of branches
as the crow flies where you're waiting, getting heavy.

Leaf, a stem in the pool,
I slept a planet long before the river

On the edge of a skylight
the woman tore a flower like a cabbage
Often she was full of beets

Now let the sun happen,
afternoon rigid with buses

One could not identify the dogsound
coming from the street just then
but a skylight if the branches had some blossoms
at the eye took shape

The weathervane shifts andante
Just tell me what you dreamed
above the winter time

Now Spring and auctions
remind you of objects, remind you of names
for things left out: Little china
gun racks, calendars, lace

sets of dishes, ships, chrome table
underneath the night we lay with
stemware, soupbowls, salt dips,

hobnail opalescent   You white rooster
on the roof's peak, you also odd-lot
mirrors, linens, lusterware

I'm out of stamps but write to you
from bed the weathervane
ventures around sometimes allegro
as when the leaves collect

Invisible the sign says
on the Carnival we're looking at
about to prepare the pelvic floor
like Horace's story about the skinny fox

who found a chink in the closed-up bin
and crawled inside to eat the corn
and what the weasel said, which was not
"I'll answer your questions about my place in the country"

Just tell me the prediction
of the weathervane raising a ruckus

pianissimo, abundant
territory
prepared for singular exchange

Seven

Alphabet

And
being
capable
does
enter
freely,
gives
howsoever.
If
less
means
nascence
or pardon,
radical
sorrow
teaches
us.
Vagabond
wanting,
Xtreme
yes: Zenith.

Calendar

To be saying of summer,
light flaws the potatoes
culled beside the piano.
To put in the compost so many apples
we fastened our pearls with a safety pin,
traveled fugue-like out of our body.
Other body ringing backward, soft pencil
leaded body on the paper sleeping body in Italian.
Darken the roses dried on the lamppost,
thud thud in the weather
all trembling kissed my mouth.
Two sisters like two arrows,
a note on the door.
As fur came in so thickly on the horses
by the fenceline, winter now.

Horoscope

When you remember the rain on the water will harm you
a river's abstract in a storm
though the Hudson was green after grief
like a nest knocked down from an eave

A swarm of wasps could touch you more kindly

Markt by the spoke of a cheap umbrella, an orchid
keeps growing in a blue vase
though its petals are brittle and break my knees
in the cart that carries the river and also the bread

In confusion I called you grass-eyed
mule on the cobblestone unlost to harm
In retrospect I slept with my children
named for the Five Positions

loosed from their papery acts

Mercurial

It's not a halfway point
we heard of in the dark
pretend tornado on the lawn: I sheltered
what you wished of me the flight risk,
added up the thin trees one by one,
their braided hair, their smoky teeth

I should already have told you—dulcet, seminal
the weather childed by storm
to storm I counted from the porch
a sort of pattern through the screen
so fastened here, so quick
sister at the stove,
a rickety porcelain stove atop a stair,
her feathered boots, her noisy hen

You should already convince me—twine,
pots, see 1999 appt. book,
all supplies—stakes, etc., straw bales
like castlerock but see-through
under cover of the clouds pretend are angels
made of snow, of lists
the things you want: the whole shebang, a trapezoidal
skyrise in a hurry, windmill with a donkey and a pear

Thesis

Everything is alchemy, Shelley said,
if it is secret

          as when you were driven
          past the smokestacks
          in your mother's car   from the window
          were there fires
          nights very dark
          occasionally from the car window moon
          speeding past, falling behind   not a question
          though it asked you
          what is your body
          a distance between

Ninth Month

"The whole problem of the self in a deeper sense becomes a sort of blind door in the background [. . .] behind which, there is nothing."

The cat's favorite place between the reader and the book, or between the lovers' heads

Kierkegaard thinking of mermen, RM thinking of Keats

"The greatest danger, that of losing one's own self, may pass off as quietly as if it were nothing; every other loss, that of an arm, a leg, five dollars, a wife, etc., is sure to be noticed."

The work a list is trying to do

Sifting the vitae for stubble fields, sweeping the bathtub for shells

That shell in a shoebox called Bloody Tooth

Those footnotes called inconsistent

No, those are not my maxipads

Dissertation love poem out in the mountains

The only box of letters saved, the comic despair, the comma an end

Acid reflux, an occupied womb

Active labor like a skateboard cut in two, a wheelbarrow
being really a peasant woman on the square

Abstraction, Miss Fishman, the Sir-
Real—

"About such a thing as that not much fuss is made in the world—"

          About a winter, summer come

philosophy, "A little drunk"

a little boat

between the lines, a pear green sail

Alphabet

After the dog tossed the stiff-as-cardboard
body of the fieldmouse
childishly about,
dizzy with killing and
eager as Adam
for the next chaseable thing,
guess what? The apricot blossomed.
Here: a petal for your
indolence,
just-resting
kaleidoscopic
love.
Mark Rothko's reds remind me
not to think of apples or
organize the pink and white
peonies of childhood—
Question: what is a cat-headed owl,
ravenous for fieldmice and flowers,
suddenly alight on the kneecap-like cover of
thought?
Utter, unmade
vow. Dream I therefore
willingly,
xing paths in
yours / our ambient, equatorial
zone.

Twelve

Documentary-postcard-graffiti Collage

What was a darling now a myth
about Paradise, only much worse
      —important scribble, unstable conversion where we stayed
something something   In the narrativa of Septembre
      glass was being blown
      under the happiness   Experiment

(the rural through a sudden view)

I understood or
I understand
    who she was with
very late and *dove, dove,* remaining
documentary-unclear
    please tell me
about the civilized war [   ] vocabulary sheet / jewelry box / car in rain?

to Lake City, Mich

Wont you come now
or is this any inducement.
    How are all the folks
all well I hope as it
leaves every one here.
How is the world using
you, it is very cold here

at present.

1913

Our photos in the church-porch made transparent
by exposure over sun / what looks like
                    a printer's *f*, erotic

blots it out. the good vegetables. They are interesting and incomprehensible.
They are vaguely called the "Weeds." They serve no purpose.
That is why it is well to question them. by favour of a lie
            (with extravagant and unnatural daughters)

Because of these things I love the very
real fact   much to do here   to remove your clothes, your pin
wheeled suit, who has   covered the grass with graffiti:

                    GRASS

                            snow

& chalked-in star (we climbed the steps) who has two names, I go to visit

    (we live in a world) in which animal life

already is felt to be at hand

Event Journal

Enormous second in which the neighbor girl walks into the house
saying *Henry Henry* because her mother wants to buy some eggs
or chickens are loose in the corn

Traffic on the highway returns

Perhaps it is a paradox
an arrow keeps traveling
a hotel stays vacant
on Mont Blanc

Who is most ravaged by the mother's death:
Cash, Jewel, or Dewey Dell

"What is the nature of each thing"
A second a fiction   to be pure of heart
to be willed one thing

One winter the road stuck us all in our houses
turning to horses or daughters or fish

Sound Journal

Singular fallout the crickets moving the earth
up to the windows all night
This is the sound of the girl in the tree

A hawk got a chicken one morning
A letter came from California
full of paper and ink

like the one the electric company mistakenly received
or the sodden one from Lake Erie
it stayed open on my knees

Someone slept in a bunkbed
Someone lay down by the canal
Another shot a chicken-hawk, its brown-white wings
an arms-length each

I said do you mean anything particular
by the lack of parenthesis
where will the traffic go

Singular makeup the absence
Dear B an umbrella
was twirled in the field

Reading Faulkner

On the clearest day the gramophone fell from the wagon
The land filled with misdirection
Nowhere to go but through
I love you whispered the river
will not leave you added the buzzard
The sky sank down like a citizen
Now the land in the middle contains me
for a small price as small as an onion

Narcissa Luna

The pool appeared to keep on
coming away from.

A moonlight read its absence in the sun's face,
crying Mirror Stage.

When we knocked on the door of the neighbor
he stuttered through his moon-read lips

that we were in the wrong place: he had no sheep,
no rubies, no hay. No other

was he then, no made-up name.

Liminal

Of a lock and key my sister dreamed
the fence immersed in weeds and birth
stone waiting on the counter—how are you,
who feels better in the summer, like a fire
body him beside her? Why lie down
with no underwear without you? And she looks good
in an old stone house, like a future or the weather
forgetting as it pooled around you
how marshes lie atop the quaking bogs
where boyhood disappears, unsayable as thistle
from a lesson in a speechless room.
Surely you know some commas
would be standard in the nineteenth century,
as spiders' webs fill up with seedfluff
in the archway of our making—so her arm
curves over you, so the petals
dropping on your head are fuchsia
from the rosebush in an instant
next to waking.

Prelude

A sickliness beginning: mud new wet ground
and the air gone mild
suddenly / gradually   green shoots somewhere
trees beginning   in the twilight
ground softening
heart sickening to begin   continuous
body pressed against garment
girl carrying pitcher   ground softening to give
way to be climbed in the
sweet dreaded air

Oscura Selva

What you, shadowed forest, didn't say
about descending like a seahorse through a pool
within a pool within a sea

about the dark wood mother
hood tipped over
in the bed   The tree was painted

upside down the wolf a bonnet
on his head   the wrists were turning
underwater, were a plant

made of the sea (the paper to write on
must be scrap   the traffic in it
shaken onto felt) and called you then

the floating fell away
the spider veins stayed wrapped
around the wrist   still made the sea

evident at moments
sounds being made
Marjorie, Barbara, Ruth Sophia

recurring wearing glasses   no one told me
"La" at the back of the throat ~ newly
born ~ occasion's cry

Cannot say disaster
held at bay   not one or the other
terza rima going sledding

or try to sneak away
what needs to be thought about
contains

Barns in Snow

The sunset here, through acts of trees.
To quarrel up the boundary
green like grass: a quandary I was wishing
through you in commotion, there he
creeps across the floor. Will you listen
at the blue table, round as water worn anew—
the rushes grow—a cat crows
birdlike in the ear. Of what befell
the lust mistook
for sorrow, being tired, wish to move this
is not snow. Along the highway nor a
woman nor a bad idea. Don't be silly
like a pillow full of atoms, where to lay your
head with horses
in the happiness
Objective

Premonition

Here are my arms in a tangle of vetch,
the purple wreathy flowering
to cover crops, and cut

There is the dead horse under the sumac
in the far field

I carried the vetch to the kitchen door
between the drought
and the arc of rain

What she woke to: some other
one in the henhouse
turning to argue
sleep away

Song

In the avenue frogs
we were hearing that day. Frogs in the cornfield geese
flying south that day. Geese in the sky were crickets
turning the sky. West of us it turned down,
"things semi-real": clouds, love,
uncut corn on the boulevard.
On a ship made a bench some song beaded the day.
Sun down. Orange sky. Oh the clouds
over the corn. Oh song
and the frost to come. One turn
or break something.
Say it is mine.

Argument

As the bony branches were black against the sky
As the sky was violet nighttime blue

As the leaves were raked and the apples sworn
to fidelity and the gloves removed

As the branches made a veil
like unto bones through which the sky night
time

Before we fell from our ladders through the leaves

a green part of your eye

Before because
not a category ("No cause, Sir, no cause")

Or light held out from the branches like a pain
in the elbow, crookd arm with a veil
hung over the arm, being ready
like being ready like grass
under the body under the bones being alive

Under study of branches the leaves
fell through ladders
the daughter lied: Because

The leaves raked sure
into grass against we lay there, ungloved hands
of trees in the argument part earth part sky

Creature

If night becalmed I point to you
and thou be tied to dreaming

in a green eye, eel-green eye
closed but roving   follow

me, field me in flower
Be found

Cricket face, frog mouth, bird head
Tin shack, rattle-can, underside

Beetle leg, fish tail, cow hand
I did try

to mind you, Creature
whose domicile surfaces
frame

oh humming

        bird oh bright

assembled matter slipping past

        oh spectacle oh humming

plea for I am cost

my eyeglass in the messy birth

        Yet in this

fact of boxes brightly lettered

box by box, an instant

        nectar for attaching

from the wire to the branch

Summer is prodigal of joy the grass
& selfheal flowering in a russet husk
& other harm seeding in the kernel

I stole the dog on the highway

& leaf this lie of
husk of self and hum

& add to find you

                                        pine bough, density, brown eye

2 girls brushing their dolls' hair
A rinsed letter about the tide

Door behind the body
where my mother lives

On the edge of a marsh
the daylilies

The landlord throws horseshoes all evening
When it's too dark to see we go home

Recalled I have
the town going past, and called the seen
jackself, truck stop

Apart from the forest
the dog lies in the grass

The pretty men paint stakes
to keep the apple trees on track

Crookedly,
the dog runs toward the white
flowering don't know

Was it for this
one speaks much less?
I weighed a dollar more
in the husk of self and hum

The effort to swallow when dying
I did not see, but some of the time we are told

Nothing of nothing, said the king
like a wooden boat

on a hill of clover
handsewn

The silo was falling a stone
at a time, debris at the bottom gathering

Where a door was, rectangle is
In a blue dress the edge

was my body, of the circular
silo standing

The best thing to do is eat some mint
if you talk too much

Let the chairs sit facing each other on the porch
and the owl lamp go out

      if a wind picks up

sulphurous and in any sense tinged,
because of the season, green—

be extremely positive
like that cedar-shingled birdhouse

swinging on its tenterhook—
tra la store of grain

Last night the moon was full
when we turned around
a story in six words

    rolled a ball across the floor

the ball had a bell inside

Infinity

It was you in the roadside phlox

"Or like a human form, a friend with whom he liv'd

benevolent"

can only hold one picture at a time

      that every thing has its Own Vortex

like a sun, or like a moon, or like a starry majesty

universe of

"As when a man dreams he reflects not that his body sleeps"

perceives it roll backward behind

About the Author

Lisa Fishman is the author of *Kabbaloom* (Wyrd Press, 2006), *Dear, Read* (Ahsahta Press, 2002) and *The Deep Heart's Core Is a Suitcase* (New Issues Press, 1998). With Henry Morren, James Fishman-Morren, and Richard Meier, she lives in Chicago and on a farm in Orfordville, Wisconsin. She teaches at Columbia College, Chicago.

Ahsahta Press

SAWTOOTH POETRY PRIZE SERIES

2002: Aaron McCollough, *Welkin* (Brenda Hillman, judge)
2003: Graham Foust, *Leave the Room to Itself* (Joe Wenderoth, judge)
2004: Noah Eli Gordon, *The Area of Sound Called the Subtone* (Claudia Rankine, judge)
2005: Karla Kelsey, *Knowledge, Forms, The Aviary* (Carolyn Forché, judge)
2006: Paige Ackerson-Kiely, *In No One's Land* (D.A. Powell, judge)

NEW SERIES

1. Lance Phillips, *Corpus Socius*
2. Heather Sellers, *Drinking Girls and Their Dresses*
3. Lisa Fishman, *Dear, Read*
4. Peggy Hamilton, *Forbidden City*
5. Dan Beachy-Quick, *Spell*
6. Liz Waldner, *Saving the Appearances*
7. Charles O. Hartman, *Island*
8. Lance Phillips, *Cur aliquid vidi*
9. Sandra Miller, *Oriflamme*
10. Brigitte Byrd, *Fence Above the Sea*
11. Ethan Paquin, *The Violence*
12. Ed Allen, *67 Mixed Messages*
13. Brian Henry, *Quarantine*
14. Kate Greenstreet, *case sensitive*
15. Aaron McCollough, *Little Ease*
16. Susan Tichy, *Bone Pagoda*
17. Susan Briante, *Pioneers in the Study of Motion*
18. Lisa Fishman, *The Happiness Experiment*

Ahsahta Press

MODERN AND CONTEMPORARY
POETRY OF THE AMERICAN WEST

This book is set in Apollo MT type with Frutiger titles
by Ahsahta Press at Boise State University
and manufactured on acid-free paper
by Boise State University Printing and Graphics, Boise, Idaho.
Cover design by Quemadura.
Book design by Janet Holmes.

AHSAHTA PRESS
2007

JANET HOLMES, DIRECTOR
CHRISTOPHER JAMES KLINGBEIL
ERIK LEAVITT
JANNA VEGA
ALLISON VON MAUR
ABIGAIL L. WOLFORD